A CLASS DIVIDED

Books by William Peters

A Class Divided

For Us, the Living (with Mrs. Medgar Evers)

The Southern Temper

Passport to Friendship: The Story of the
Experiment in International Living

WILLIAM PETERS

A CLASS DIVIDED

DOUBLEDAY & COMPANY, INC.
GARDEN CITY, NEW YORK
1971

Photographs by Charlotte Button.
For the ABC News documentary
program *The Eye of the Storm.*

Library of Congress Catalog Card Number 78–154704
Copyright © 1971 by William Peters
All Rights Reserved
Printed in the United States of America
First Edition

For Jane Elliott and her third-grade class
of 1970:

John Benttine	Tammy Bill	Verla Buls
Sandra Dohlman	Susan Ginder	Raymond Hansen
Greg Johanns	Rex Kozak	Laurie Mayer
Donna Reddel	Russell Ring	Brian Saltou
Sheila Schaefer	Julie Smith	Roy Wilson
	Milton Wolthoff	

ACKNOWLEDGMENTS

I am grateful to the American Broadcasting Company and particularly to Thomas H. Wolf, of ABC News, for permission to make use in this book of material gathered on an assignment undertaken for them. Readers interested in the documentary film that resulted from that assignment—*The Eye of the Storm*—should direct inquiries to American Broadcasting Company Merchandising, Inc., 1330 Avenue of the Americas, New York, N.Y. 10019.

Montauk, New York   *William Peters*

A CLASS DIVIDED

I

On any normal weekday morning, Jane Elliott looked forward to getting to her classroom at the Riceville, Iowa, Community Elementary School and to the teaching job she loved. Eager to pick up the threads of the previous day's lessons, delighting in her third-graders' sense of wonder at anything new, she saw each day as a kind of adventure in the company of children she enjoyed. Often she was reluctant, when the day was over, to see them leave. Not infrequently, they felt the same way. Once they had seriously proposed that the entire class spend the night at school.

But that Friday in April, 1968, was not a normal morning. The day before, Martin Luther King had been murdered in Memphis. For Jane, that had suddenly made a lot of things different. She had made a decision about what she would do in her class, a decision that now

11

made her reluctant to leave the house for school.

Her husband, Darald, was perfectly capable of seeing that their four children were properly fed and dressed for school before he left for his own job. He did it often when she had a particular reason for getting to the school a little early. Yet today she fussed about the kitchen, urging one child to eat and another to change his shoes, sipping at a second cup of coffee—knowing that she was only stalling.

Finally, with a glance at her watch, she shrugged into a jacket and said good-by. Darald, who knew what she was planning winked at her and then smiled encouragingly. She grimaced at him as she went out the door.

She had made her decision, and she would stick to it, though she dreaded what she felt sure lay ahead. For a while, at least, she would be making each of her twenty-eight students unhappy; for a time, all would dislike her and resent what she was putting them through. She had worked hard since September to establish a warm and trusting relationship with each of them, and she had been proud of their success as a class in becoming a happy, co-operative, productive group. What she was now going to do would strain those hard-won ties, perhaps even threaten them. It was hardly a pleasant prospect.

Still, driving her car through the quiet, early-morning streets, she refused to give in to her

growing sense of apprehension. She had to do
something if she was any kind of teacher at all.
She refused to do something that was essen-
tially meaningless. What she had thought of
promised at least a chance of being an effective
lesson. Nor was there time now to plan anything else. Whatever was to be done would
have to be done today, while the shock of Dr.
King's brutal assassination still reverberated in
the mind.

She had made her decision in horror and
anger and shame the night before as she sat
on the living-room floor ironing the stitched
sheets of an Indian tepee and watching the television coverage of the aftermath of the murder.
That decision had stood the test of the
dawn's colder appraisal, and she was not going
to permit a faint heart to change it.

The things she had planned to teach inside
the giant tepee would now have to wait, she
decided, for all of them had paled beside the
urgent message that had burst from her television set the night before. Now, the senseless-
ness, the irrationality, the brutality of race
hatred cried out to be explained, understood,
committed irrevocably to memory in a lesson
that would become a part of the life of each
child she could reach with it.

That was what she had struggled half the
night to devise; it was what she had finally
thought of: a lesson that might accomplish just
that. She knew that her children would ask

about the murder, that they had undoubtedly
watched what she had watched. They had already discussed Martin Luther King in class.
Now they would have to discuss his violent
death. But this time, they would do more than
that. Much more.

Setting aside her doubts, she opened the door
of Room 10, turned on the lights, and went to
her desk. As she sat down, she saw before her
the Sioux prayer she had planned to teach the
children after they had erected the giant tepee:
"Oh, Great Spirit, keep me from ever judging
a man until I have walked a mile in his moc-
casins." It was precisely the lesson she hoped
to teach today, though not at all in the way she
had contemplated. First, she thought unhappily, they are going to have to walk that mile.

It began, really, even before the bell rang.
A boy came into the room bursting with the
news. "They shot that King yesterday!" he said
excitedly. "Why did they shoot that King?"

"We'll talk about that," Jane promised, and
after the opening exercises, they did. When
everyone had had a chance to tell what he
knew, Jane asked them what they had heard
and what they knew about Negroes. In the tiny
town of Riceville, population 898, and the
sparsely settled farming area surrounding it,
there were no Negroes. In the school's text-
books, like those in so many American schools,
Negroes were neither mentioned nor pictured.

Whatever her children said, then, Jane assumed would have come from parents, relatives, and friends, from what they had learned in school —in her own class and in the grades before— and from things they had seen and heard in a rare movie or on the radio or television.

Rather quickly, a pattern developed from their answers. Negroes weren't as smart as white people. They weren't as clean. They fought a lot. Sometimes they rioted. They weren't as civilized. They smelled bad.

None of it was said in a vicious way. There was no venom, no fear, no hate, but rather a sort of disapproval, a sense of disdain. Some of the children quoted parents to back up points, though there was no real argument. It was as though their teacher had asked them to describe a vaguely unpleasant experience they had all shared. They told what they knew about Negroes calmly, reaching back in their memories for details, corroborating each other, expanding on each other's points. Behind her expression of friendly interest, Jane was appalled.

She asked them to define the words "prejudice," "discrimination," "race," "inferior." That was not difficult; they had discussed these concepts before. Then they talked about some of the things Negroes in various parts of the United States were not permitted to do. Finally, Jane asked them if they could imagine how it would feel to be a black boy or girl.

"This they discussed at some length," Jane

Elliott says now, "and eventually, they decided
that they could. Now, in spite of the things they
had 'known' about Negroes, they became sympathetic. They felt sorry for black children; they
didn't think it was fair for them to be treated
differently. And they had had enough of the
subject. Dr. King's death had been adequately
disposed of. I could easily have stopped right
there.

"Yet all I could think of as I saw this attitude
of sympathetic indifference develop was the
way I had myself reacted to racial discrimination all these many years: Sure, an incident can
anger you. Sure, you feel sorry about the way
blacks are being treated. Sure, something ought
to be done about it. And now, what shall we
talk about?"

But Jane Elliott's identification with the children in her class went deeper. Raised, like
them, on a farm near Riceville, growing up in
the all-white, all-Christian community, she had
herself lived in the midst of the kinds of prejudices they had expressed in their descriptions
of Negroes. Though she had long since re-
jected those prejudices, there was still much
that she could see of herself as a child in the
children who sat now at their desks in front
of her. She had once been there, too, and was
now, at the age of thirty-five, looking back
through all the years that had intervened. What
she saw—even in her own strong, yet inactive,
opposition to racism—was simply not enough.

"I felt desperately," she says, "that there had to be a way to do more as a teacher than simply tell children that racial prejudice is irrational, that racial discrimination is wrong. We've all been told those things. We know them, at least in the sense that we mouth them at appropriate times. Yet we continue to discriminate, or to tolerate it in others, or to do nothing to stop it. What I had racked my brain to think of the night before was a way of letting my children find out for themselves, personally, deeply, what discrimination was really like, how it felt, what it could do to you. Now the time had come to try it."

What happened next in Jane Elliott's classroom was, as far as she knew, a product of her own mind. She had never heard of anyone else who had done it. She was not even sure it was a good idea. She knew only that she had to do something, and this was all she had thought of to try.

The idea went back to a half-angry, half-humorous remark she had made to a college roommate years before. Returning to school after a weekend in Riceville, she had told her roommate about an argument she had had with her father on the subject of race. Remembering as she talked about it how her father's hazel eyes had blazed at her accusations of prejudice, she told her roommate, "If hazel eyes ever go out of style, my father's going to be in trouble."

She had no sooner said it than it struck both girls as an interesting observation. Skin color, eye color, hair color or texture: it made as much sense, they decided, to discriminate on the basis of one as another. The two of them talked far into the night about how it must feel to be a Negro in America.

Jane Elliott never forgot that discussion. Later, when she and Darald were married and he became the assistant manager of a supermarket in the Negro section of Waterloo, Iowa, she saw his Negro customers and employees as different from herself only in this: they knew, as she didn't, how it felt to be the object of prejudice, hate, and fear. Everything else she learned about Negroes convinced her that they were basically no different than whites.

Then, with Darald suddenly transferred to another city, Jane had been faced with the problem of renting their house. A real estate agent and neighbors cautioned her not to rent to blacks. She paid little attention until a woman telephoned in response to an ad. "She asked if the house was for whites or colored," Jane says, "and suddenly those warnings sprang into my mind. I hesitated a moment and then said that all of my neighbors were white. She said, 'Oh, well, thank you anyway,' and hung up, and I stood there with the telephone in my hand feeling as though I had defected to the enemy.

"For a long time after that, I felt like a snake.

I knew what I should have done—I should have
said the neighborhood was white but that she
could come and look at the house if she were
interested. But, of course, I hadn't. I tried to
analyze why I had evaded the issue, and I was
forced to the conclusion that I had backed away
from my principles out of fear of my neighbors'
opinions. If we had rented to a Negro family
and later wanted to move back, we would have
had to face their anger. I saw that when the
chips were down, I had not been able to face
that. And I hated myself for it."

It was after that experience that Jane began
to read about the racial crisis in America. One
of the books she read was John Howard Grif-
fin's *Black Like Me*, the story of a white man's
experiences in the South with his skin dyed a
deep brown. Here was a man who had found
out what it was like to be a Negro, and Jane
suffered with him the thousand daily insults,
the inconveniences, the fears, the wounds to
pride that Southern Negroes experience in the
course of simply going about the business of
living.

Then, suddenly, on the night of the day that
Martin Luther King was murdered, all of these
memories and experiences had coalesced into
an idea of how she might give her third-graders
a sense of what prejudice and discrimination
really meant.

Jane took a deep breath and plunged in. "I

don't think we really know what it would be like to be a black child, do you?" she asked her class. "I mean it would be hard to know, really, unless we actually experienced discrimination ourselves, wouldn't it?" Without real interest, the class agreed. "Well, would you like to find out?"

The children's puzzlement was plain on their faces until she spelled out what she meant. "Suppose we divided the class into blue-eyed and brown-eyed people," she said. "Suppose that for the rest of today the blue-eyed people became the inferior group. Then, on Monday, we could reverse it so that the brown-eyed children were inferior. Wouldn't that give us a better understanding of what discrimination means?"

Now there was enthusiasm in their response. To some, it may have meant escape from the ordinary routine of a school day. To others, it undoubtedly sounded like a game. "Would you like to try that?" Jane asked. There was an immediate chorus of assent.

II

Divided by eye color, Jane Elliott's class was
made up of seventeen children with blue eyes,
three with green eyes, eight with brown eyes.
To make the groups more even, the green-eyed
children were lumped with the brown-eyed.
Because those with blue eyes still outnumbered
the others—and because Jane's bright blue eyes
might tend to make things a little easier for
them—she had decided that they should represent the minority group the first day.

"Today," she told the class, "the blue-eyed
people will be on the bottom and the brown-
eyed people on the top." At their puzzled looks,
she went on. "What I mean is that brown-eyed
people are better than blue-eyed people. They
are cleaner than blue-eyed people. They are
more civilized than blue-eyed people. And they
are smarter than blue-eyed people."

When they still looked puzzled, Jane nodded shortly. "It's true. It really is."

Now the brown-eyed children began to look at each other in wonder. They sat up straighter in their chairs, waiting to hear more. The blue-eyed children frowned, stirred uneasily, not understanding. One blue-eyed boy slumped way down in his chair. "What color are your eyes?" Jane asked him.

"Blue," the boy said, straightening up.

"Is that the way we've been taught to sit in class?"

"No," the boy said.

"Do blue-eyed people remember what they've been taught?" Jane asked the class. There was a chorus of "No's" from the brown-eyed children as they began to see how it would work. The blue-eyed boy now sat bolt upright, his hands folded neatly in the exact center of his desk. A brown-eyed boy near him, one of his close friends in the room, gave him a withering, disdainful look. It began that quickly.

The rules for the day were enumerated to the growing delight of the brown-eyed children and the increasing discomfort of the blue-eyed. Brown-eyed children could use the drinking fountain in the room as usual. Blue-eyed children were to use paper cups. The brown-eyed children would have five extra minutes of recess. They would go first to lunch, could choose their lunch-line partners, and could go back for seconds. The blue-eyed children could do none of these things.

"Who should sit in the front of the room?" Jane asked.

"The brown eyes!" shouted the brown eyes.

"Who should be our row leaders?"

"The brown eyes!" they shouted again.

At her nod of approval, there was a great tumult of sound and motion as the children pushed their desks and chairs to the new positions.

The blue-eyed children winced and squirmed as the list of rules grew longer. "Blue-eyed people are not allowed to play with brown-eyed people unless they are invited," Jane told them. "They may not play on the big playground equipment at recess. And they may not take the small playground equipment out of the room."

With the rules established, Jane swung quickly into the day's regular schoolwork. When a brown-eyed child stumbled in reading aloud, she helped him. When a blue-eyed child stumbled, she shook her head and called on a brown-eyed child to read the passage correctly. When a blue-eyed boy, tense and nervous, rolled a corner of a page of his reading book into a tight curl as he awaited his turn to read, Jane displayed the book to the class. "Do blue-eyed people take care of the things they are given?" she asked.

23

"No!" shouted the delighted brown-eyed children.

That was the way it went. The brown-eyed children took a special joy in baiting their blue-eyed classmates. None invited their erstwhile friends to play with them at recess. One lovely and brilliant blue-eyed girl, among the most popular children in the class, almost disintegrated under the pressure. She walked in a slouch, became suddenly awkward, tripped twice over things, did poorly in her work. At recess, walking disconsolately across the playground, she was struck across the back by the deliberately outstretched arm of a brown-eyed girl who the day before had been her best friend.

"You got in my way," challenged the brown-eyed girl, "and I'm better than you, so you have to apologize."

Abjectly, the blue-eyed girl mumbled an apology. The other girl walked away in triumph.

"Long before noon," Jane says now, "I was sick. I wished I had never started it. During the morning recess, I went to the teachers' lounge and told three other teachers what I was doing. They laughed. I went back to my empty room and cried.

"By the lunch hour, there was no need to think before identifying a child as blue or brown-eyed. I could tell simply by looking at them. The brown-eyed children were happy,

alert, having the time of their lives. And they
were doing far better work than they had ever
done before. The blue-eyed children were miserable. Their posture, their expressions, their
entire attitudes were those of defeat. Their
classroom work regressed sharply from that of
the day before. Inside of an hour or so, they
looked and acted as though they were, in fact,
inferior. It was shocking.

"But even more frightening was the way the
brown-eyed children turned on their friends of
the day before, the way they accepted almost
immediately as true what had originally been
described as an exercise. For there was no question, after an hour or so, that they actually believed they were superior. The fact that we
were going to change roles on Monday was forgotten. Everything was forgotten in the face of
the undeniable proof that the blue-eyed children were inferior to them. It was as though
someone had pointed out to them something
they simply had not noticed before. Weren't
the blue-eyed children making more mistakes
than they were? Of course. Wasn't the teacher
finding fault almost exclusively with the blue-
eyed children? Of course. Wasn't it clear that
she liked the brown-eyed children better? Of
course. What better proof did you need?

"Sometime that day, I pulled down a roller
map at the front blackboard. As I let go, it flew
back into its case with a great clatter. It was
something I had done before. As I turned dis-

gustedly to pull it down again, a brown-eyed girl in the front row said, 'Well, what do you expect? You've got blue eyes.'"

Startled, Jane recovered her composure before she turned back to the class. "Is that why I did that?" she asked. There were nods of agreement from several brown-eyed children. Then a blue-eyed boy came to her defense. "Naw," he said. "She's never been able to pull it down right."

That brought up the question of her status as a teacher, for if she had blue eyes and was, hence, inferior, how could she teach brown-eyed children? "I have a better education," she told them. "I've been to college. And even though I may not be as smart as brown-eyed people, I'm better educated than brown-eyed people who haven't been to college."

"That's right," said a brown-eyed boy. "She knows more than brown-eyed kids, but she's not as smart as the brown-eyed teachers in the school."

"Why do you think I'm just a teacher and not the principal of the school?" Jane asked, wondering just how far they would carry this line of reasoning.

"Because Mr. Brandmill has brown eyes!" cried a brown-eyed girl with pride. Dinsmore Brandmill was the school's principal.

Jane shrugged her shoulders in mute agreement, wondering now what color Mr. Brandmill's eyes really were.

III

Before the end of school on Friday, Jane Elliott reminded the children of how the day had
begun. "We decided to try this," she said, "to
see if we could learn something about discrimination. And we said that on Monday, the
brown-eyed people would be on the bottom
and the blue-eyed people would be on top.
We'll talk more about that on Monday, but I
want to remind you that that's the way it's going to be."

Four hands shot up, and Jane called on a
brown-eyed boy. "If you're going to do that,
I'm not coming to school," he said. "Neither am
I," said a brown-eyed girl. "Me neither," said
another.

"How many of you think you're coming to
school Monday?" Jane asked. All but the three
who had spoken raised their hands, though
other brown-eyed children were slow to re-

spond. "All right. We'll see who's here on Monday." Then, turning back after a quick glance at the clock, Jane noticed the looks of pleasure at the promise of revenge on the faces of many of the blue-eyed children. "Do you blue-eyed people think you're going to enjoy Monday more than you did today?" she asked.

"Yes!" they shouted, laughing.

"Well, we'll see about that, too. But it's still Friday now, and it's time to go home. So get the things off your desks, and when the bell rings, the brown-eyed people may go first to their lockers and line up first for the buses. And remember, when you get on the buses, you blue-eyed people are to sit as far to the rear as you can." The bell rang as she finished, and in a few minutes, the school day was over. Jane, exhausted, sank into the chair at her desk in the empty classroom, trying desperately to sort out her impressions of what had happened, still horrified at much that she had seen, wishing once more that she had never started it, but knowing, with a sense of dread, that she would have to go through the whole thing again on Monday.

Over the weekend, she half-anticipated telephone calls from some of the parents or from Mr. Brandmill. No one telephoned. She told her mother and father what she had done, how the children had responded, and she could see that her father was shaken at the description of the way the brown-eyed children had behaved toward their blue-eyed classmates.

"It was a lonely, scary weekend," she says. "I talked and talked and talked about what had happened, not only to my parents but to Darald and my two sisters, who had been teachers. I couldn't get it out of my mind. And I couldn't help feeling very much alone. I had done this on my own, and whatever happened, I was solely responsible. At home, I caught myself looking at my own four children, wondering how I would feel if a teacher did to them what I had done to my class. I thought I would approve, but I couldn't be sure. And then, suddenly, I found myself wondering if my children would have behaved as my third-graders had. I had no answer to that at all."

On Monday, all of the children in Jane's class came to school. She made no mention of the three who had said they wouldn't come. Briefly, she recalled to them all what they had done on Friday and how it had begun. Then, as the blue-eyed children became restless and fidgety, she said, "I lied to you on Friday. I told you brown-eyed people are better than blue-eyed people. That's not true."

There was an expectant hush. "The truth is that blue-eyed people are better than brown-eyed people. They are smarter than brown-eyed people. They are . . ."

She guessed, as she went through the entire

list for the second time, that there might now be greater resistance to what she was saying. Perhaps, having been fooled once, they would simply have no more of this nonsense. Yet, watching their faces carefully, she saw that it was having an effect. The faces that had been gleeful on Friday were rapidly falling into depressed scowls. Those that had been glum on Friday brightened with pleasure. To make sure that she was getting through, she tossed off the names of famous people, asking, as though it were generally known, what color their eyes were. The blue-eyed children came through as expected. "Blue!" they cried happily with each new name.

As Jane continued reversing Friday's procedure, reviewing the restrictions that today would apply to the brown-eyed children, a number of blue-eyed boys and girls gloated visibly at the prospect of revenge. The changing of the seating was accomplished quickly, and the reminder signs that had been placed on the drinking fountain and paper cups were reversed. Almost at once, Jane began finding fault with brown-eyed children.

"I had not expected that the brown-eyed children, knowing full well after their experience on Friday that it was all an exercise and that it would last only a day, would react as intensely as the others had to the experience of discrimination," Jane says now. "But they did. Within minutes, they had become nervous, depressed, resentful. The only real difference that day was that the blue-eyed children, now on top, were noticeably less vicious in their treatment of the underlings than the latter had been to them.

"I speculated about the reason for this, but I could only guess why. Was it because a whole weekend had intervened? Was it because they were in the numerical majority even when they were being discriminated against and felt that there was somehow safety in numbers? Or was it just possibly because, having experienced discrimination themselves, they were able to identify with the 'inferior' group and felt sorry for them? Naturally, I hoped it was the last, though I couldn't be sure."

Toward the end of that day, Jane ended the exercise, telling the class that it had all been a lie. She asked them what they had learned and was heartened by their answers. "Does the color of your eyes have anything to do with what kind of person you are?" she asked.

They literally shouted their answer at her. "No!"

The tensions of the two-day exercise broke like a dam giving way to a flood, and she laughed with them, comforted those who cried with relief, and nearly cried herself at the sight of boys who had been separated by the color of their eyes wrestling happily together, of girls, eyes wet with joy, hugging friends they had thought forever lost.

On Tuesday, Jane led a wide-ranging discussion of what they had learned. There was little need to encourage the children to contribute; all were bursting with things to say. Finally, with the air completely cleared, Jane asked each child to write a composition defining "discrimination," describing how he had felt on each of the two days, and telling who Martin Luther King was. When the papers had been corrected for spelling and punctuation, they were read aloud to the group.

"Discrimination," Julie Kleckner wrote, "is being judged by the color of your skin or the color of your eyes or the church you go to." Carol Anderson wrote, "Discrimination is a word for when a person is judged not by what he does but by the color of his skin. I found out what it feels like in school." Dale Brunner put it more personally. "Discrimination," he wrote, "is happy and not happy."

Brown-eyed Sindee Hockens, having defined discrimination, went on to write: "Our room heard about it when Martin Luther King died and we wanted to see what it felt like to be a Negro child, with black skin. The brown-eyed children were the whites and blue-eyed children were the Negroes. This was Friday. I have brown eyes. I was happy. The brown-eyed children were hot-shots; I felt good inside.

"On Monday, I felt mad because I was being discriminated against. The blue-eyed people got to be first in line and the teacher just ex-

plained to the blue eyes their mistakes and
bawled us brown eyes out. I was sick."

Debbie Anderson, also brown-eyed, said of
Monday, "I felt mad and I wanted to tie the
people with blue eyes up and quit school because they got to do everything first and we had
to do everything last. I felt dirty. And I did not
feel as smart as I did on Friday. Discrimination
is no fun. Martin Luther King did not like discrimination against Negroes."

"On Monday," brown-eyed Dale Brunner
wrote, "I could have locked them in jail because I was mad. The blue-eyes got to be first
in the lunch line, and got to be first in lunch,
and got five extra minutes of recess. I didn't
want to work. I didn't feel like I was very big.
Discrimination is no fun at all. I am glad I am
not a Negro and being judged by my skin."

Theodore Perzynski described the two days:
"On Friday, we practiced discrimination. The
brown-eyed people got to do things first. I have
blue eyes. I felt like slapping a brown-eyed person. It made me mad. Then I felt like kicking
a brown-eyed person. I felt like quitting school.
The brown-eyed people got five extra minutes
of recess.

"On Monday I was happy. I felt big and
smart. Then we got five extra minutes of recess.
We got to do everything first. And we got to
take out the playground equipment. I do not
like discrimination. It makes me sad. I would
not like to be angry all my life."

Dennis Runde, blue-eyed, wrote, first, of Friday: "The people with brown eyes could do almost anything. The people with blue eyes could not do half the things the people with brown eyes did. I felt left out because I have blue eyes. I felt like giving them all black eyes."

Of Monday, Dennis wrote: "On Monday, April 8, we had Discrimination Day again only the people with blue eyes got to be the wheels. Boy, was that fun! We got to do all the things first. That was living it up. I felt like I was smarter, bigger, better, and stronger."

Bruce Fox's contribution was succinct: "Discrimination is being judged by your skin color. On Friday, the people with brown eyes got to have a recess and art and I have brown eyes. I was happy. We did the same things on Monday except the people with blue eyes got to have long recess and p.e. [physical education] and I felt like blowing the teacher sky high."

Nor was there any question that the children knew who Martin Luther King was. "Martin Luther King wanted Negroes to have what they wanted just as white people do," Carol Anderson wrote. "And he was killed for doing this. He was killed by discrimination."

Billy Thompson wrote: "Martin Luther King died trying to save colored people from discrimination. White people at least could treat colored people like any other people."

IV

When all the papers had been read, Jane recalled for her third-graders the things they had
said about Negroes before the exercise began:
that they weren't as smart, as clean, or as civilized as white people; that they fought and
rioted; that they smelled bad. Some of the
things they had written in their compositions
now came back to them with new force:

Debbie Anderson: "I felt dirty."

Sindee Hockens: "I was sick."

Dale Brunner: "I didn't feel like I was very
big."

Debbie Hughes: "I felt like quitting school."

Billy Thompson: "I felt like crying."

Dennis Runde: "I felt left out."

Theodore Perzynski: "I felt like kicking a
brown-eyed person."

Kim Reynolds: "I felt like being a drop-out."

One by one, the children examined what they

had felt to be true of Negroes in the light of their own experiences. Was it possible, Jane asked, that being accused of being careless almost from the day you were born might tend to make you something less than careful? Is being told again and again that you are not as clean as another person likely to give you a positive attitude toward cleanliness?

If you know that no matter how hard you work, you will be called dumb because your eyes are the wrong color, will that make you want to try your hardest and do your best work? If you feel angry or sick or left out because of discrimination against you in school, are you going to want to go to school? Is it easy to keep your mind on schoolwork when you know that others are looking down on you because of the color of your eyes?

Each question sparked a discussion; each discussion led further toward a conclusion. Discrimination not only hurt, it affected the way you behaved. The way you behaved affected not only the kind of work you did, it affected the way you felt about yourself. The way you behaved, the kind of work you did, and the way you felt about yourself—all these affected the way you appeared to other people; in fact, they could affect the way you actually were. Discrimination could change the kind of person you were if it went on long enough. And there was another conclusion: it was no better—and no more accurate—to judge a person by the color of his skin than by the color of his eyes. Neither told you anything important about the person.

"Before we were through," Jane says, "I was convinced that the children had learned a great deal from the exercise and that it was learning that would stick. And though there had been no thought on my part that the exercise was an experiment from which I might learn, I felt when it was over that I had learned more than the children had.

"I learned far more than I wanted to know about the effect of being considered superior and what reactions it could trigger in nice, average, middle-class, white American children. All of the children enjoyed being considered superior, and the feeling that they were had obviously pushed them to do better work than they had ever done before. But some of them took a savage delight in keeping the members of the 'inferior' group in their place, in asserting their 'superiority' in particularly nasty ways. I had not seen this side of my students before, nor was I really aware of its existence, at least in them. I was wholly unprepared for their lack of compassion for people they normally considered their best friends.

"I wasn't prepared, either, for the degree of anger and rebellion expressed by every child at becoming a second-class citizen. During our discussion on Tuesday, for example, it came out that there had been long, serious conversations

on the playground and in the boys' and girls'
rooms about what the 'inferior' group would
like to do to me. It ranged from throwing things
at me to killing me. Nor had I realized until I
saw it how destructive a feeling of inferiority
really is, how it can literally change a personal-
ity, how it can drag down efficiency, destroy
motivation.

"During those two days, the atmosphere in
the classroom changed from one in which the
children felt mutual respect and even admiration for each other to one in which the tension
from feelings of contempt, greed, conceit, frus-
tration, envy, and despair was almost unbear-
able. We were all glad it was over, but what we
had seen of ourselves and each other, what we
had felt either as 'superior' or 'inferior' people,
what we had learned, not only intellectually
but in a deeply emotional way as well—all these
left their imprint on everyone in that classroom,
students and teacher as well."

From the beginning, Jane had conceived of
the exercise as a classroom lesson for her third
grade and nothing else. Yet, as it proceeded—
and particularly after it was over—she began to
anticipate some kind of response from outside
Room 10. What had happened was too explosive, too deeply moving for word of it not to
reach someone who had not been there. The
three teachers in the teachers' lounge had
laughed that first day, but perhaps others, hear-
ing about it, would at least want to know more.

She had expected that at least one parent might telephone, either to complain or to praise, and that if she did not hear about it directly, she would hear from Mr. Brandmill, the principal. None of these things happened. It was as though the entire exercise had been conducted in the strictest secrecy.

"When I told Mr. Brandmill what I had done," Jane says, "he expressed interest. When I described how the children had behaved, he was surprised. I had a feeling that he thought they had been pretending, acting out roles assigned to them by the teacher like good little boys and girls. It was then that I first realized how difficult it would be to make anyone believe what had actually happened. You almost had to *be* there, to see it as it was going on, to know that the children, far from acting, had somehow accepted the situation as real despite the fact that it had been presented to them as unreal."

With her father, Jane had greater success. Describing what had happened in great detail, she could see that he felt the children's wounded pride, their hurt feelings, their acceptance of an imposed status of inferiority as an almost personal blow. He was appalled at the behavior of the "superior" group. "Before this," Jane says, "my father, though he would never have hurt anyone, held many of the same beliefs about Negroes that my third-graders had expressed before the exercise. I could al-

most see those beliefs eroding in the days after
the exercise as we discussed it again and again.
It affected his views deeply."

When word of Jane's unique lesson in discrimination did finally get out, it was because
of the admiration of a close friend of what she
had done. Among the people her friend told
was Merritt Messersmith, owner and publisher
of the Riceville *Recorder*, a twelve-page
weekly. Messersmith, fascinated, wanted to
know more, and two weeks after the classroom
exercise, he published a story, along with ex-
cerpts from some of the children's compositions.

If the *Recorder*'s news story had an impact
in Riceville, Jane Elliott did not feel it. Close
friends, who had known what she had done,
mentioned the story. Then she heard that it had
been picked up by a wire service. That, Merritt
Messersmith could not resist telling her with a
certain pride. Then, finally, came a reaction,
though not at all what Jane had expected.
Johnny Carson telephoned and asked her to
come to New York to appear on the "Tonight"
show. "I didn't quite know what to make of
that," Jane says, laughing, "but I went."

After her appearance, mail began to come in
from all parts of the country. It continued,
sporadically, throughout the summer. Most was
favorable, though some was ugly. But the most
interesting response for Jane came, finally, from
the mother of one of the girls in her class, and

it was not to the television show but to what had happened in the classroom.

They met by accident. The girl's mother said, "I want you to know that you've made a tremendous difference in our lives since your Discrimination Day exercise. My mother-in-law stays with us a lot, and she frequently uses the word 'nigger.' The very first time she did it after your lesson, my daughter went up to her and said, 'Grandma, we don't use that word in our house, and if you're going to say it, I'm going to leave until you go home.' We were delighted. I've been wanting to say that to her for a long, long time. And it worked, too. She's stopped saying it."

V

When school began again in the fall, there were in Jane Elliott's new third-grade class a number of children who needed special help in reading. Selected by their former second-grade teachers as those in their classes who were farthest behind in learning to read, these children were, for the first time at the school, placed as a group in a single third-grade classroom. Jane, after completing a course in remedial reading at Rochester, Minnesota, had volunteered to take them.

From the beginning, she made it a point to talk frankly with these children about their reading problems, to point out that they could be solved, to convince them that they were not dumb, as they might have thought or even been told they were, and to promise them that, together, she and they would soon prove it. By the middle of the year, they had.

But long before that, at the very beginning
of the school year, Jane had tried to face the
question of whether she should repeat her classroom lesson in discrimination. There was no
question, ever, of wanting to. It was too unpleasant. But there was the more important
question of whether she felt it to be a valuable
exercise for the children. On balance, she had
decided it was, but the presence in her classroom this year of boys and girls who were—and
who knew they were—far behind other children
their age in reading, called for special consider-
ation.

It could be assumed, she felt, that any child
with reading problems at the third-grade level
had already tasted in his home or in school
some of the bitterness of being thought inferior. A good part of her work with these children was, in fact, based on the conviction that
they must lose whatever sense of inferiority
they had acquired before they could be expected to profit fully from the special meth-
ods of learning to read that she used with
them. To burden them with the additional
weight of actually being treated as inferior,
even for just a single day, raised obvious
questions.

There were other factors to be considered.
"One of the first things I had worried about,"
Jane says, "after seeing the delight with which
the first year's class practiced discrimination
when they were in the 'superior' group, was

1. Of her unique lessons in discrimination, teacher Jane Elliott says, "I wanted my third-graders to learn about discrimination from the inside, by experiencing it. I hope when they are involved, later on, in similar situations, they will recognize what the other person must be feeling—and pull back."

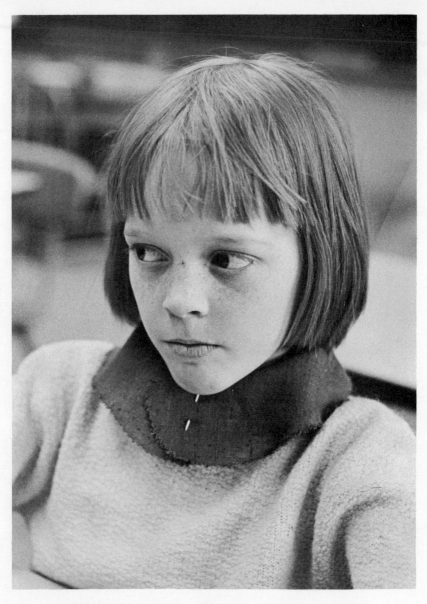

2. Julie Smith wears the collar symbolizing membership in the "inferior" brown-eyed group.

3. The happy blue-eyes go first to lunch. Front to rear: Raymond Hansen, Greg Johanns, Brian Saltou. Unhappy brown-eyes, wearing collars and denied second servings, follow: Laurie Mayer, Verla Buls, John Benttine, Donna Reddel, Julie Smith, Sandra Dohlman, Roy Wilson.

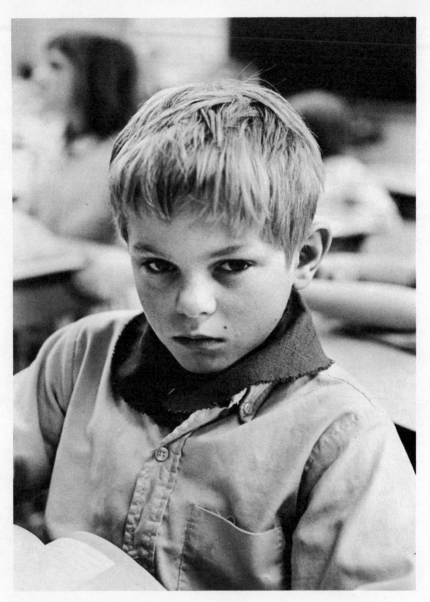

4. After a recess scuffle on the playground, John Benttine admits under questioning, "Russell called me names, and I hit him. Hit him in the gut." The names Russell called him: "Brown-eyes."

whether I might be teaching the joys of discriminating along with the horrors of being discriminated against. It's a real question. I had decided, finally, that it had just not worked that
way, because for the two remaining months of
school that year, whenever we discussed it—and
the children brought it up again and again—
no child ever indicated a willingness to repeat
the exercise even for another chance at being
on top for a day. What they remembered, what
they talked about, and what they applied to
other situations, was not how good they had
felt when they were treated as superior but the
misery of being treated as inferior. That and the
pain of being separated from friends, which of
course happened on both days."

Nor was this all that gave Jane pause when
she considered whether or not to repeat the exercise. "I was far from eager to go through the
experience again myself," she says. "It ranked
high in my memory of most unpleasant chores,
and I had felt after it was finally over that first
time that I would never do it again. It's hard
work, for one thing, probably because it forces
a teacher to do deliberately what she normally
tries hardest to avoid: to deceive her students, to tell them something she knows is not
true. It's a complete reversal of ordinary good
teaching. And besides that, you work and work
to build up a good rapport with your students,
and then for two days you deliberately destroy
it, knowing you will somehow have to build it

up again when the lesson is over. That hadn't
taken long to do with the first group; inside of
half an hour, we were all good friends again.
But how could you be sure it would work that
way with a second group? And with every
child?

"Finally, there's the simple fact that it's a
sickening experience to cause children with
whom you've identified closely that much pain,
even if you're convinced that the lesson is important. I had felt like a monster picking on a
child I would normally help, singling out for
ridicule a child I would normally protect from
it. I had flinched inside myself every time I did
it. I had had to force myself to pick up the cues
the children provided me with. I had wanted
to call it off a hundred times each day. And I
had kept wanting to say to the class, 'What's
wrong with you? Why don't you stand up and
refuse to put up with this? Why don't you de-
fend each other from me?'

"Yet even as I had thought that, I had
known that I represented authority in that
room, that they had all been taught from birth
to respect authority, and that this was at least
a part of the reason they didn't resist. And isn't
that at least part of the reason that racial discrimination persists in this country? Didn't the
segregation laws in the South and don't the cus-
toms of discrimination in the North represent
the same kind of authority to adult Americans?
How many of us stand up to them? And this,

too, is a valid part of the lesson, it seems to me: that it is healthy to question authority when you know that it's wrong. Isn't that what Martin Luther King's life—and death—were all about?

"Still," Jane says with a deep sigh, "there must be a better way to teach children these lessons than the one I thought of. There must be a way to keep children from growing up into the kind of adult so many of us are, a way less drastic, less painful than this. And if we can get to the moon, we can certainly find it. There must be an expert somewhere who could tell me a better way to do this job. But so far, nobody has."

And so, in the end, Jane led her second class through the exercise that had come by now to be called "Discrimination Day." Convinced after a month with them that all of the children could handle the problems presented by it, even more convinced on the basis of the first year's results that it was an important part of the learning process, she scheduled the lesson in October, giving herself most of the school year to observe and deal with the results.

What happened during those two days was similar to what had happened the previous year, though there were some differences. One boy, for example, maintained consistently throughout the entire exercise that eye color made no difference in people. "It's not true," he said whenever Jane made a discriminatory statement. "It's not fair," he insisted whenever she gave one group an advantage over the other. When his own group was given extra recess, he still maintained that it was not right.

"You should be happy, Paul," Jane told him. "You have the right color eyes."

"But it's not true and it's not fair no matter what you say," he replied heatedly.

A second boy seemed simply to ignore the entire exercise. Without openly objecting to it, he simply proceeded to treat his friends of whatever eye color as he always had. He didn't discriminate; he wasn't depressed at being in the "inferior" group or elated at being in the "superior" group.

Because she had this class for nearly eight months after the exercise, Jane was better able to observe the long-term effects of it than she had been with the first year's group. "All through the year," she says, "they applied what they had learned to new and different situations. When the question of how we could have 'Peace on Earth' arose at Christmas time, Paul, the boy who had resisted Discrimination Day from beginning to end, said, 'We can have it by making all the grownups go through Discrimination Day.'

"Another time, when they all came in from recess, there was grumbling about the teacher who had been on playground duty. It had been going on for some time, so I asked them about it. Whether they were right or wrong I don't know, but almost all of them stoutly maintained

48

that the teacher was always picking on the same group of boys from another third-grade classroom. 'They don't do anything wrong,' one boy said, 'but every time we go out, she just watches those same kids and bawls them out for nothing.' The others agreed. Then one child said, 'She's discriminating against them. That's what she's doing.' And suddenly everyone had the same idea: the teacher should go through Discrimination Day. Then she'd know how it feels."

When word got out that Jane had held her exercise again, a group of high school boys who rode the same school bus as several of her third-graders began taunting the youngsters. "You're the kids that have that nigger-lover for a teacher," they jeered. "You must all be nigger-lovers in that class."

"These were the older boys my third-graders had looked up to and admired and envied for three years on that same school bus," Jane says. "They were the noisy, boisterous, tough group that sat in the back of the bus each morning and afternoon, and they had always seemed quite glamorous to my young boys. But when this happened, one of my boys came strutting into the room as though he were suddenly ten feet tall. 'Boy, Mrs. Elliott,' he said, 'did I learn something on the bus this morning!' I asked him what he had learned, and he said, 'We already know more than those high school kids do. They were calling us "nigger-lovers" on the bus today. We already know that it's wrong to use the word "nigger," and we know that there's nothing wrong with being one, either. And they're in high school, and they don't even know that!'

"I was torn between guilt and pride: guilt at having exposed these nine-year-olds to such taunts and pride at their response. Because the others agreed with him."

Some weeks after the exercise, the mother of one of Jane's third-grade boys met with her at a conference. "What have you done with my son?" she asked. "He's a different boy at home. We actually look forward to his getting off the bus at night. He even treats his little brother and sister kindly. He just doesn't act like the same boy at all. What happened to him?"

"It was true," Jane says. "I had seen the same change in him at school, and it dated from Discrimination Day. From a belligerent, overbearing, unpopular boy, he had become a thoughtful, pleasant child. Almost overnight. And while he was certainly an exception in the sense of such a dramatic change, all of the children seemed to me to be more loving and much kinder to each other than before. The whole attitude in that room changed after the exercise; we were all much more comfortable with each other."

VI

Jane Elliott's success in teaching remedial reading led, the following year, to a class of sixteen third-graders, all of whom had difficulty with reading. For a while, that fall of 1969, she wondered again whether she dared to introduce the lesson in discrimination. Keeping an open mind about it, she turned to her work with her usual enthusiasm.

Late in the fall, with the whole class making good progress, she decided she would give the lesson, scheduling it mentally for about the middle of the year. That would give her time to establish a good relationship with each of the children before it happened and time, afterwards, to allow the children to elaborate on whatever they learned from it.

In a way, when the time came, it was as though the two previous experiences had been a sort of dress rehearsal, for meanwhile ABC

News had asked permission to send a producer and two complete camera crews to film the lesson for a network television documentary. That meant that this time whatever happened in the classroom would be ineradicably recorded on film, and an audience of millions of Americans would see it.

Arrangements for the filming were made without difficulty. Mr. Brandmill, the school principal; Donald Johnson, the superintendent; the school board; the parents of the children in the room—all gave their approval. The children, however, were told only that their class had been chosen to be filmed for television. They had no warning—and presumably no knowledge—of the Discrimination Day exercise to come.

To give the eight boys and eight girls in the class a chance to get used to the lights, cameras, microphones, and film crews—and to give the producer an opportunity to film normal school activities—it was decided to film an entire day before the exercise began. Cameras and lights were set up in the classroom on a Sunday, and when the children arrived on Monday, February 23, Room 10 had been transformed into a miniature sound stage. All equipment had been placed along one side of the room, leaving Jane and her children free to use the rest of the room as they normally would.

Jane had previously cautioned the children not to look at the cameras and to ignore the activities of the camera crews. With few exceptions that first day, they did. She had also discussed with them the fact that the filming was to take place during Brotherhood Week and asked them to think about what that meant. As it happened, two members of the eleven-man crew were Negroes. The children seemed scarcely to notice.

That Monday passed quickly, both for the children and the film crews. During recess, at the lunch hour, and before and after school, the children chattered excitedly with the producer and his assistant, the two cameramen and their assistants, the three soundmen, and the electricians. They watched cameras being loaded and unloaded, looked through the lenses, tested the microphones, and listened to their voices on the tape recorder. A piece of film, a length of audio tape became prizes to take home and show the family.

When class was in session, the crews went about their work silently and unobtrusively, filming and recording the high points of the day. Cameramen who had filmed everything from riots to earthquakes, soundmen who had recorded prize fighters and Presidents, and a producer of documentaries on civil rights in Mississippi and wild animals in East Africa—all were quickly drawn into the interplay between teacher and students, for Jane Elliott had a zest for her work and a delight in her third-graders that was fascinating to watch. And, of course, the film crews, unlike the students, knew what was going to happen the following day.

The cameras were rolling when, during that day, Jane asked each child to draw a picture of her. As they bent to the task, glancing up frequently at her, a girl in the back of the room asked what color her eyes were. "Blue," Jane said, removing her glasses for a moment. "What color are yours?"

"Brown," the girl said, opening them wide.

"I wonder," Jane said casually, "how many of us have brown eyes." The drawing stopped, and the children peered at each other's eyes. When a count had been made, there were eight with blue eyes and eight with either brown or green eyes. Jane wrote the names and the eye colors on the front blackboard. Then everyone went back to his crayons. When the drawings were finished, Jane collected them. Without exception, they pictured her with a broad smile. She wondered, paging through them, how the brown-eyed children would portray her tomorrow.

Their names and eye colors were still on the blackboard when the children entered the brightly lighted room the next day. Before the bell rang, several children drifted over to where the camera crew stood quietly beside their equipment. The men were accepted now as part of the classroom, and there was little of the previous day's excitement about their presence.

The day began with the salute to the flag.
During the singing of "God Bless America,"
which Jane led spiritedly from the front of the
room, Raymond Hansen, a handsome boy with
fair hair, bright blue eyes, and the soft, round,
angelic face of a choirboy, turned almost unconsciously toward the rest of the room and,
singing lustily, kept time with one hand. He
was clearly a child who enjoyed school.

"Who knows a poem?" Jane asked as soon as
they were seated. Hands shot up, and for the
next ten minutes there were eager recitations
interspersed with songs that various children
suggested. Brian Saltou, a puckish boy with an
infectious grin, recited "Little Orphant Annie"
from beginning to end with hardly a stumble
and then smiled with pleasure at his accom-
plishment.

Finally, Jane glanced at the calendar on the
front wall and said, "This is a special week.
Does anybody know what it is?"

"National Brotherhood Week," several children responded.

"What's 'brotherhood'?" Jane asked.

There was a pause and then Sandra Dohlman, a quiet child with an appealing, waifish
look, asked hesitantly, "Be kind to your
brothers?"

"Okay," Jane said, nodding. "Be kind to your
brothers."

"Treat everyone the way you would like to
be treated?" Raymond Hansen asked.

"Treat everyone the way you would like to be treated," Jane repeated. "Treat everyone as though he were your—"

"Brother," the class said in unison.

Jane took a few steps toward the door and then turned to ask, "Is there anyone in the United States that we do not treat as our brothers?"

"Yeah," several children answered.

"Who?"

Raymond Hansen answered instantly. "Black people."

"The black people," Jane said. "Who else?"

"Indians?" asked Sandra.

"Absolutely, the Indians," Jane said. "And when many people see a black person or a yellow person or a red person, what do they think? What do they sometimes say?"

Sandra made a disgusted face. "Ew, look at the dumb people," she said.

"Look at the dumb people," Jane said flatly. "What else do they think sometimes? What kinds of things do they say about black people?"

Greg Johanns, a stocky boy with an alert air, frowned and said, "They call them 'Negroos,' 'niggers,' things like that. When I used to say 'Negroes,' my father said I should call them black people. You're supposed to call them black people now."

Jane nodded and went on. "In the city and in many places in the United States, how are black people treated? How are Indians treated?

How are people of a different color than we are treated?"

Greg Johanns was back with an answer. "Like they're not part of this world. They don't get anything in this world."

"Why is that?" Jane asked.

"Because they're a different color," Greg replied.

When Jane asked them what they knew about black people, several children volunteered answers. "They're big," one boy answered, "the ones you see playing football on TV."

Donna Reddel, a tall girl with large brown eyes and straight brown hair, said she thought some of the black women on television were pretty, and she named a Negro singer. "I like her hair," she added.

"Some of them have hair out to here," a boy said, describing an Afro haircut with his hands.

Donna said, "Yesterday, some of the kids in the hall said, 'You have two niggers in your room.' I told my mother last night we had two black people in our room." She glanced quickly at the two Negro members of the film crew.

"Did you tell your mother anything else about them?" Jane asked.

Donna grinned. "I said I liked them."

Jane nodded. "Greg said we treat black people differently because they're a different color. Do you think that's true?"

"Sure," Raymond said.

"Do you think you know how it would feel to be judged by the color of your skin?"

There was a thoughtful silence, and then Rex Kozak, a short, wiry boy with blue eyes and blond hair, nodded. "Yeah," he said doubtfully.

"Do you think you do?" Jane asked again. Several of the children shook their heads. "Do you think you know how it would feel to be a black boy or girl in a school with mostly white children?" This time there were more head-shakers. "No," Jane said, "I don't think you would know how that felt unless you had been through it, would you?"

Now there was general agreement. Jane paused. "Would you like to know?"

There was a scattering of yesses from the class. "Well, let's see," Jane said. "Is there anything about you people that is different from one another that we could use to make part of you—"

"Black?" Raymond asked, before she could finish.

Jane pursed her lips noncommittally.

"The eyes!" a girl said suddenly. "The color of the eyes!"

"Okay," Jane agreed. "We could use the color of your eyes. How many in here have blue eyes?" Eight hands shot up. "Okay," Jane said, "how many in here have brown eyes—or green?" The hands of the other eight went up.

"It's all right there on the blackboard behind

you," a girl said, pointing, and Jane turned to look at the list.

"That's right, it is." She turned back to the class. "It might be interesting to judge people today by the color of their eyes," she said speculatively.

Three children began bouncing up and down in their seats with excitement.

"Would you like to try this?"

"Yeah!" The answer was almost a shout as the entire class was caught up in enthusiasm for the idea.

"It sounds like fun, doesn't it?" Jane asked.

"Yeah!" the whole class shouted again.

"All right. Since I'm the teacher, and I have blue eyes, I think maybe the blue-eyed people should be on top the first day."

Roy Wilson, a serious-looking boy with brown eyes, close-cropped hair, and a long, oval face, frowned with puzzlement. "You mean . . ." He stopped, unsure what she could mean.

"I mean," Jane said with finality, "the blue-eyed people are the better people in this room."

"Uh-uh!" It was Brian Saltou, his blue eyes flashing.

"Oh, yes, they are," Jane said, turning to face him. "Blue-eyed people are smarter than brown-eyed people . . ."

"Uh-uh!" Brian said again, even more forcefully. "My dad isn't stupid."

"Is your dad brown-eyed?" Jane asked.

"Yep," Brian said bluntly.

"One day you came to school and you told us that he kicked you," Jane said. There were snickers from the rest of the class.

Brian grinned and nodded, just once. "He did."

"Do you think a blue-eyed father would kick his son?" Jane asked.

"My dad would," Brian said definitely.

Jane shrugged. "My dad's blue-eyed, and he's never kicked me. Raymond's dad is blue-eyed, and he's never kicked him. Russell's dad is blue-eyed, and he's never kicked him."

Brian refused to listen. Putting his hands on his head, he jammed his arms against his ears and put his head down on his desk, ignoring her.

"What color eyes did George Washington have?" Jane asked.

Sandra Dohlman and Julie Smith, both brown-eyed, seated alongside each other, turned at this to stare at each other's eyes. "Blue?" Sandra asked, blinking, clearly hoping she was wrong.

Brian's head was up again. "Blue," he said disgustedly, "or else brown."

"Blue," Jane said. "Blue." She paused. "This is a fact. Blue-eyed people are better than brown-eyed people."

Brian shook his head vigorously.

"Are you blue-eyed or brown-eyed?" she asked him.

"Blue."

"Then why are you shaking your head?"

He shrugged his shoulders. "I don't know."

"Are you sure that you're right?"

He nodded once with complete assurance.

"Why? What makes you so sure that you're right?"

"I don't know," he said, and without saying it, his expression added: *but I am.*

Jane turned back to the rest of the class, and the children, who had followed the argument closely, twisted back in their seats to face the front of the room again. "Today," Jane said, when it was evident that no one else was going to contest her statements, "the blue-eyed people get five extra minutes of recess, while the brown-eyed people have to stay in."

There was a gasp of delight from the blue-eyed children, a low moan from the brown-eyed.

"The brown-eyed people do not get to use the drinking fountain," she continued. "You'll have to use the paper cups."

"Why?" asked Donna Reddel, her brown eyes wide with annoyance.

Jane repeated the question to the class. "Why?"

Greg Johanns had the answer. "Because we might catch something from them?"

Jane looked at him and nodded shortly. "We might catch something from you." She paused to let it sink in. "You brown-eyed people are not to play with the blue-eyed people on the playground, because you are not as good as blue-eyed people. You cannot play with them unless you are specifically invited to."

A number of the brown-eyed girls looked plaintively at their blue-eyed friends. "And I would suggest," Jane added, "that you blue-eyed people think twice about it before you invite a brown-eyed person to play with you today. You may not mind playing with a brown-eyed person, and you may if you wish, but you'll probably want to think about what your blue-eyed friends will think of you."

In the hush that followed, Jane moved to her desk at the back of the room. "The brown-eyed people in this room today are going to wear collars so that we can tell from a distance what color your eyes are." She picked up eight blue felt collars and a box of pins from the desk. "We aren't always close enough to see your eyes, and we want to be able to tell even when your back is turned," she said, walking back to the front of the room. "We wouldn't want to make a mistake. Now the blue-eyed people, each of you can pick out someone on whom to put a collar. So blue-eyed people each come up and get a collar."

"I will!" cried Sheila Schaefer, the only one of an inseparable threesome of girls to have blue eyes. She hesitated only a moment between her two best friends, dark-haired Susan

Ginder and slim, freckled, red-haired Julie
Smith. Then she pinned the collar on Julie.

The other blue-eyed children busied themselves pinning collars on their brown-eyed classmates, but Brian Saltou remained in his seat.
When Jane held out the last remaining collar,
he got up reluctantly and took it, pinning it on
the only brown-eyed child left without one.
Then he took his seat again.

VII

After the blue-eyed children had been given seats in the front of the room and the job of row leader in each row had been reassigned to a blue-eyed student, Jane told them to get out their English workbooks. "Turn to page 127," she said, writing the number on the blackboard.

"Is everyone ready?" she asked finally, glancing around the room. "Everyone but Laurie," she said, watching brown-eyed little Laurie Mayer squirm as she paged rapidly through her workbook. "Ready, Laurie?" she asked when Laurie had found the page. Laurie nodded, looking up unhappily through her harlequin glasses.

"She's a brown-eye!" someone jeered.

"She's a brown-eye," Jane confirmed. "You'll begin to notice today that we spend a great deal of time waiting for brown-eyed people."

Laurie pursed her lips unhappily, and Donna, sitting near her, flashed a brown-eyed, resentful look at Jane.

That was the way it went all morning. Whenever a brown-eyed child was slow, whenever one made a mistake, Jane made a point of picking it up. Blue-eyed children could seemingly do no wrong. As the brown-eyed children became tense and unhappy, the blue-eyed children relaxed and all but blossomed under the approving eye of their teacher. All but Brian Saltou. Brian, who had objected so strenuously at the outset to Jane's insistence that blue eyes made you better, still seemed part of neither group. He neither taunted the brown-eyed nor identified with the blue-eyed. Jane had always seen him as a kind of loner. He remained one.

At morning recess, the blue-eyed children were excused five minutes early, and they left the room in a bustle of enthusiasm. Brian went along without a visible sign of special pleasure. The brown-eyed children remained behind, working gloomily at their desks. When it was time for them to go out, they pinned their collars to their coats and trudged morosely out to the snowy playground, sullen, disgruntled, angry children. Three brown-eyed girls marched fiercely across the playground, avoiding the crowded swings, slides, and jungle gym, giving a wide berth to clusters of playing children. Their heads together, they talked furiously as they stomped briskly the length of the frozen yard.

Two brown-eyed boys slipped around a corner of the building and seated themselves, alone, on a step against the brick wall. By the time recess was over, all of the brown-eyed children had found each other and were huddled in little groups along that wall. Two girls consoled a third, who was close to tears.

It was after recess when Russell Ring, a large, good-natured, blue-eyed boy, explaining how he had got so wet, said that he had been wrestling. "You like to wrestle, don't you?" Jane asked, smiling.

"Sure," Russell said.

"He's strong, too," Rex Kozak said, laughing.

"Well, of course he's strong," Jane said. "He's got blue eyes. You must be strong, too, Rex."

"Sure," Rex said, "but not as strong as Russell."

Blue-eyed Greg Johanns, sitting next to Rex, said, "I like to fight, too. You should see what I can do to my little sister."

Jane laughed out loud. "Greg, you're always fighting with your little sister, aren't you?"

Greg smiled and nodded. "Sure. It's fun."

Later that morning, Jane, sitting with a blue-eyed reading group at a round table in the back of the room while the other children worked at their desks, reached behind her to the chalk tray for a yardstick to use as a pointer. It wasn't there. "The yardstick's gone," she said, looking quickly around the room. "I don't see the yardstick, do you?" she asked the children in the group. When one of them found it and brought it to her, she took it and stood up at the blackboard.

"Hey, Mrs. Elliott!" Raymond Hansen said excitedly. "You better keep that on your desk so if the brown people—the brown-eyed people —get out of hand . . ." His voice trailed off.

"Oh," Jane said, unable to keep a note of disapproval out of her voice, "you think if the brown-eyed people get out of hand, that would be the thing to use?"

A number of brown-eyed children had turned around to look resentfully at Raymond. Raymond backed down. "Well, no," he said.

At lunchtime, Jane stood in front of the class. "Who goes first to lunch?" she asked.

"The blue-eyes," said those with blue eyes.

"The blue-eyed people," Jane agreed. "No brown-eyed people may go back for seconds. Blue-eyed people may go back for seconds. Brown-eyed people do not."

"Why not the brown-eyes?" Brian asked with more than a trace of annoyance in his voice.

"Don't you know?" Jane asked him.

"They're not smart," Greg Johanns informed him.

"Is that the only reason?" Jane asked the class.

5. The next day, with the brown-eyes designated "superior," blue-eyed Russell Ring is collared by Donna Reddel, who laughs, "I've been waiting all day to put this on Russell!"

6. Brown-eyed Susan Ginder smiles delightedly when Jane Elliott points out to a blue-eyed child who had forgotten his glasses, "Susan Ginder has brown eyes. She didn't forget her glasses."

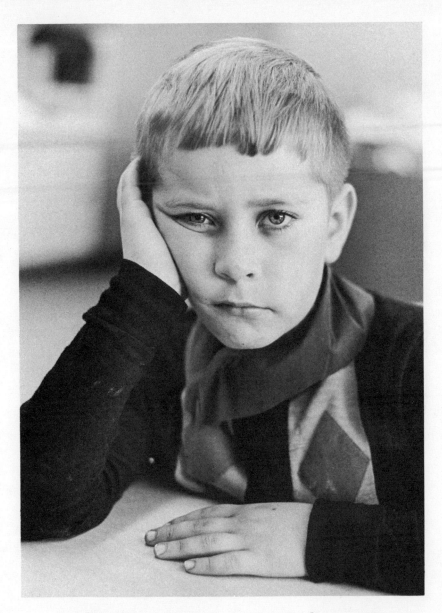

7. Blue-eyed Raymond Hansen, an eager discriminator the first day, turns glum when the rules are reversed. On top: "I felt like a king, like I ruled the brown-eyes. Like I was better than them. Happy." On bottom: "I felt down, unhappy, like I couldn't do anything, like I was tied up and couldn't get loose."

8. Alone of the children, Brian Saltou resisted at every step the idea that either group was superior. Singled out for Mrs. Elliott's scorn on his "inferior" day, he waited until she looked away, then mouthed a silent message more eloquent than any curse.

"You're afraid they'll take too much," Sheila
Schaefer said gleefully.

"They might take too much," Jane said, nodding. "Now let's get in line, the blue-eyed people first."

As the children moved to form a double line
at the door, Raymond spoke up. "You should
tell the person that you go back to for dessert
to watch for these collars."

Once again, Jane had difficulty concealing
her annoyance at Raymond's delight in discriminating against his brown-eyed classmates.
"Oh," she said finally, "you think I should alert
the lunchroom help to know that these people
should be treated differently?"

"The woman that you go back to for seconds!"
Greg shouted. "Tell her! Tell her!"

Sheila Schaefer, securely in the front of the
line with the other blue-eyed children, jumped
up and down excitedly. "Yeah!" she squealed.
"Yeah!"

"Probably we should do that, shouldn't we?"
Jane asked.

There was a chorus of yesses from the front
of the line.

During the afternoon recess, there was a brief
scuffle between big, jolly, blue-eyed Russell
Ring and John Benttine, smaller, quieter, and
brown-eyed. John's anger at what had been
happening had been smoldering inside him for
hours. Even though he and Russell were close

friends, he was clearly unwilling to be taunted by him.

Jane, having heard about the fight, brought it up as soon as recess was over. "What happened at recess?" she asked. "Were two of you boys fighting?"

"Russell and John were," several children reported at once.

"What happened, John?" Jane asked.

His chin all but buried in the collar around his neck, John looked up resentfully. "Russell called me names, and I hit him. Hit him in the gut."

"What did he call you?"

John's lips quivered as he answered. "Brown-eyes."

"Did you call him 'brown-eyes'?" Jane asked Russell.

Russell looked up sheepishly at her through his glasses.

"They always call us that," Roy Wilson complained from across the room.

" 'Come here, brown-eyes,' that's what they say," Verla Buls said, imitating the jeering cat-call.

"They were calling us 'blue-eyes'," Rex Kozak said.

"I wasn't," Susan Ginder said.

"Me and Sandy and Donna were," Roy Wilson admitted.

"Yeah," Rex agreed.

"What's wrong with being called 'brown-eyes'?" Jane asked the class.

"It means that we're stupider and—well, not that exactly," Roy Wilson said.

Before he could continue, Raymond, blue eyes bright with excitement, interrupted. "Oh, that's just the same as other people calling black people 'niggers'!"

Turning back to John, Jane asked him, "Is that the reason you hit him?" John stared at her, his brown eyes smoldering. He nodded shortly.

"Did it help?"

John shook his head.

"Did it stop him?"

He shook his head again.

"Did it make you feel better inside?"

Once more he shook his head, this time reluctantly.

Turning to Russell Ring, Jane asked, "Did it make you feel better to call him 'brown-eyes'?" Russell looked embarrassed, but he didn't answer. "Why do you suppose you called him 'brown-eyes'?"

Now Brian entered the discussion. "Why, because he has brown eyes," he said, as though anybody could see that.

"Is that the only reason?" Jane asked. "He didn't call him 'brown-eyes' yesterday, and he had brown eyes yesterday, didn't he?"

"But we just started this," a brown-eyed girl objected.

"Yeah," Brian said accusingly. "Ever since you put those blue things on them," circling his neck with a finger to indicate the blue collars the brown-eyed children wore.

The final blow for the brown-eyed children that day came when Jane sent their blue-eyed classmates off to gym without them. When the others had left the room, she faced eight scowling children. "Let's all come down here to the front of the room," she said, perching on a stool between the desks and the blackboard. They came, reluctantly, and sat on the front desks or on the floor.

"How do you feel about today?" Jane asked them.

"Awful," Donna Reddel said.

"Terrible," said red-haired Julie Smith.

"It hasn't been a very pleasant day, has it?" Jane asked. They agreed that it hadn't. "Why?"

"Because we've got brown eyes," Roy said.

"Have you learned anything today that you didn't know before?"

For a moment there was only a glum silence. Then Sandra Dohlman spoke. "It's better to have blue eyes," she said miserably.

"Can you do anything about the color of your eyes?"

Sandra shook her head.

"You can't change them, can you?"

They all shook their heads.

"Do you wish you had blue eyes?"

"Yes," several of them answered.

"Why?"

"Well, because you get to go to recess early," Susan Ginder said.

"And you get seconds at lunch," Laurie Mayer said.

"And you get to go to gym," Julie Smith added.

"And why is that?" Jane asked.

"Because you have blue eyes," a number of them responded.

"And that's the only reason?"

"Blue eyes are better," Sandra said. "They get everything."

"And we have to wear these stupid collars," Donna said angrily.

"If you took the collars off, would that change anything?" Jane asked.

"No," several of the children said.

"Why not?"

"Well, we'd still have brown eyes," Susan Ginder said.

"That's right," Jane said. "Brown eyes are the problem, aren't they?"

A number of them nodded morosely.

"You remember when we started this, we said we'd like to find out how it feels to be discriminated against. Do you think you know now how it feels?"

"We sure do," Roy said.

"How does it feel?"

"It feels awful."

"You feel like you can't do anything," Julie Smith said.

"I feel mean," Donna said.

"It's like you don't have any friends anymore," Verla Buls said, picking at her collar.

"Would you like to take these collars off?" Jane asked.

"Yeah," they all said dubiously, not quite daring to hope.

"Take them off." The collars were off in no time. Jane collected them. "I lied to you today," she said. "It wasn't true when I said that blue-eyed people are better than brown-eyed people. That's not true at all. Brown-eyed people are every bit as good as blue-eyed people."

"Yeah," Roy said, brightening.

"They are," Jane said. "And tomorrow, the blue-eyed people are going to find out how it feels to be discriminated against for the color of their eyes."

"You mean they're going to have to wear those stupid collars?" Donna asked, still suspicious.

Jane nodded, and Donna's face was transformed by a wide grin. "And you're going to have five extra minutes of recess while they stay in," Jane added.

Donna licked her lips in anticipation. "Oh, boy!"

"Boy, are we going to show them!" Roy exclaimed, throwing his arm over John's shoulder. John, who had said little since the fight at re-

74

cess, smiled slightly, and then withdrew into himself again. The other children wriggled with excitement.

"Are you looking forward to tomorrow?" Jane asked.

"Yeah!" they answered.

"Are you going to treat them the way they treated you today?"

"Yeah!"

"How did they treat you today?"

"Awful," several of them said.

"And that's how you're going to treat them tomorrow?"

This time the response was less enthusiastic.

"Do you remember how you felt today?"

They nodded.

"And that's the way you want them to feel tomorrow?"

"Well, it's only fair," Donna protested. "They were mean to us today. Now it's our turn."

"That's right," Sandra said. "They did it first."

"So tomorrow you're going to give it right back to them, is that it?"

"Well, why not?" Donna asked.

Julie Smith shrugged her shoulders. "Maybe not as bad as they did," she said.

"But you do want them to know how it feels, is that right?"

The dilemma was clear on most of their faces. They wanted to get even, to have their revenge, but they knew there was something wrong in it.

"Well, but can't we at least have extra recess and all that?" Laurie Mayer asked plaintively. "They got that."

"Oh, you're going to have all the privileges they had today," Jane said. "I'm just wondering how you're going to treat them. They treated you badly, and I wonder if you're going to treat them badly, too."

Susan Ginder, who with Julie Smith had lost the company of their best friend, blue-eyed Sheila Schaefer, that day, had not failed to note Sheila's delight in discriminating against both of them. She was intent on fighting back. John Benttine, who had fought over being called "brown-eyes," was clearly so glad this day was over that he had little room in his thoughts for the next one. Perhaps, by defending himself, he also felt that he had had his revenge.

"How many of you think you're going to give the blue-eyed people a bad time tomorrow?" Jane asked. Most of the hands went up, though there was something tentative about some of them. "Well," Jane said, "it will be interesting to see what happens tomorrow."

"They won't like it," Verla Buls said thoughtfully.

"No, I'm sure they won't," Jane agreed. Then, glancing at the clock, seeing there was still time before the others returned from gym, she asked, "Did you believe me when I told you that blue-eyed people were better than brown-eyed people?"

Four or five of them said yes. Others shrugged.

"Did you think it might be true?"

Now nearly all of them nodded.

"Why?"

"Well," Roy said slowly. "You told us."

"But why did you believe me?"

There was silence.

"Would you have believed me if I'd told you the moon was made of green cheese?"

"No," they said, shaking their heads.

"Then why did you believe this?"

Donna said, "I didn't know whether to believe you or not at first, but then, later, it seemed like it was true."

"Why?"

"Well," Sandra said, "because we just couldn't do anything right today."

"Oh," Jane said. "So when I told you you weren't as good as they were, you didn't feel as good anymore. Is that it?"

Roy nodded. "I just couldn't think straight today."

"Why?" Jane asked. "Because you have brown eyes?"

"No," Roy said with finality.

"Then why?"

"Well, because we had to wear those collars and . . ."

"Because you were picking on us all day," Donna said flatly. "That's why. I told Verla I was going to tell my mother tonight that you'd been mean to us all day. I wasn't going to come to school tomorrow."

"Neither was I," Verla said.

"Do you think now you'll come to school?" Jane asked with a smile.

"I sure will!" Donna said, smiling broadly. Everybody laughed.

Before the others returned to the classroom to be dismissed for the day, Jane cautioned the brown-eyed children on the need for secrecy about what she had told them. "We don't want them to know until tomorrow what's going to happen," she said, "so you will all have to act sad when they come back and on the bus tonight and on the bus tomorrow morning. Do you think you can do that."

Eight beaming faces tried desperately to look unhappy.

"You'll have to do a lot better than that," Jane said, laughing at them.

VIII

They came into the classroom next morning looking much as they had the day before: the blue-eyed children cheerful, breezy, self-confident; the brown-eyed children lethargic and solemn. Only occasionally, in a glance or a nudge, as the brown-eyed children pinned their collars on again and took their seats, could their suppressed excitement be glimpsed.

When the opening exercises were over, a blue-eyed boy spoke up. "I know what's going to happen today. My brother told me you're going to turn it around."

"Oh, he did, did he?" Jane said.

"Yes. He said you're going—"

"Just a minute," Jane said, and the boy stopped. She looked away from him and at the rest of the class. Donna had a hand clasped across her mouth, hiding a grin. "Yesterday," Jane said, "I told you that brown-eyed people aren't as good as blue-eyed people. That wasn't true. I lied to you yesterday."

Brian Saltou shook his head, shrugged heavily, and said, "Oh, boy, here we go again."

Jane ignored him. "The truth is that brown-eyed people are better than blue-eyed people."

A sprinkling of delighted laughter came from the brown-eyed children. The faces of the blue-eyed sobered. Jane, glancing quickly around the room, saw Russell Ring squinting up at her with his pale blue eyes.

"Russell, where are your glasses?"

"I forgot them."

"You forgot them. And what color are your eyes?"

He stared at her sheepishly and then looked around him, like a boy caught swimming naked. "Blue," he admitted finally. The brown-eyed children squealed with pleasure.

"Laurie Mayer has brown eyes, and she didn't forget her glasses. Susan Ginder has brown eyes. She didn't forget her glasses." Susan leaned out from her desk to smirk at Russell. He grinned with embarrassment and looked away. "Russell Ring has blue eyes, and what about his glasses?" Jane continued.

"He forgot them!" the brown-eyed children answered joyfully.

Brian Saltou, studiously ignoring the conversation, had taken a tiny model car from his desk and begun to play with it, studying its wheels intently. Jane saw him.

"All these brown-eyed people are listening to what we're saying," Jane continued. "Look at Brian." The children swung around in their chairs. "Are blue-eyed people good listeners?"

"No!"

Without a flicker of recognition that he was being talked about, Brian continued to study the car.

"Brian, will you put that down, please?" Jane asked.

Even now, he did not look up, but he slipped the car back into his desk.

"Thank you." Jane took a step toward Greg Johanns. "Yesterday, we were visiting, and Greg said, 'Boy, I like to hit my little sister as hard as I can. That's fun.'" Greg winced, putting one hand to his face as though recoiling from a blow. "What does that tell you about blue-eyed people?" Jane asked.

"They're naughty," a brown-eyed girl said.

"They fight a lot," said another.

"Are blue-eyed people as civilized as brown-eyed people?" Jane asked.

"No," the brown-eyed children answered.

"The brown-eyed people may take off their collars," Jane said, "and each of you may put your collar on a blue-eyed person."

Before she had finished, Donna Reddel, eyes dancing, her face beaming with pleasure, had whipped off her collar and was scurrying up the aisle to Russell Ring's desk. Pinning the collar around his neck, she looked up at Jane. "I've been waiting all day to put this on Russell," she chortled. Russell blushed helplessly.

Raymond Hansen, who the day before had been full of ideas of ways to discipline the brown-eyed children, sat glumly, the corners of his mouth pulled down, as a collar was pinned on him. Of all the brown-eyed children, John Benttine seemed the least anxious to stigmatize a blue-eyed child with a collar. He still had one in his hand when all the blue-eyed children but Brian Saltou wore them. Almost reluctantly, then, the boy who had fought being called "brown-eyes" crossed the room to the desk of the boy who had fought the entire exercise.

Brian sat motionless, totally without expression, as John pinned the collar around his neck. Then, as John left, he put his head down on the desk, elbows against his ears, in the position he had assumed the day before.

Jane ran quickly through the rules for the day. "The brown-eyed people get five extra minutes of recess," she said. "You blue-eyed people are not allowed to be on the playground equipment at any time. You blue-eyed people are not to play with the brown-eyed people unless you are invited . . ." Tammy Bill, a blue-eyed girl with short, straight hair, pouted unhappily as the list grew longer.

When they had changed the row leaders to brown-eyed children and it came time to move the brown-eyed children to the front of the room, Brian lifted his head from his desk and, without getting up, scraped his chair and desk backwards to the new position. Then he put his head down again, blocking out Jane's voice with his arms. In a moment, though, it was clear that he could still hear.

Jane said, "Brown-eyed people are better than blue-eyed people."

Brian lifted his elbows and banged them hard on his desk.

Jane said, "They are cleaner than blue-eyed people."

Brian banged his elbows again.

Jane said, "They are more civilized than blue-eyed people."

Once more, Brian punctuated her sentence with a bang.

"They are smarter than blue-eyed people, and if you don't believe it, look at Brian."

There was a rustle as all of the children turned to look. Brian's head was still down.

"Do blue-eyed people know how to sit in a chair?" Jane asked. "Very sad. Very, very sad."

Brian's head was up now, and he glared defiantly at Jane. As she looked away, his lips began to move in a silent message he dared not say aloud. His expression said it all. No curse could have been more eloquent.

That was the day that Greg Johanns got up quietly from his chair and went to the sink for a drink. Observing the printed sign that read

"Brown" on the drinking fountain, he took a
paper cup from the box and filled it at the tap.
After drinking, he walked to the wastebasket
and threw the cup away. He was halfway back
to his seat when Jane's voice stopped him.

"Greg, what did you do with that cup?"

He stared at her.

"Will you please go and get that cup and put
your name on it and keep it at your desk?" As
he turned to obey, she continued. "Blue-eyed
people are wasteful."

That was also the day that Russell Ring, returning from morning recess, unpinned the blue
collar from his coat, put the pin between his
lips as he hung the coat in his locker, and, when
another boy slapped him on the back, swallowed the pin. Surprised but unhurt, he hurried
to Jane. "I ate a pin," he told her.

"Are you sure, Russell?" she asked worriedly.

"Yes." He explained how it had happened.

Putting the class to work, Jane took him to
the nurse's office, where they called his mother.
Assured that he would be taken immediately
to the hospital for X-rays, she left him and returned to the class. The strain of the exercise
had already taken a heavy toll of Jane's emotions. This incident was almost too much. Worried about Russell, she wondered if she could
keep her mind on what she was doing. At the
classroom door, she had an almost irresistible
impulse to call the whole thing off. Then, know-

ing she could not abandon the lesson in the middle, she squared her shoulders and re-entered the room.

"Russell swallowed a pin," she told the class calmly, "and he's being taken to the hospital. They'll take X-rays to find out where the pin is. I'm sure he'll be all right, and I'll tell you as soon as we have news of him."

The children accepted her explanation quietly, and Jane quickly put them to work. John Benttine, at the blackboard to write a contraction, was given a brief lesson in making a proper W. When he had mastered it, Jane said, "Now, that's beautiful writing! Brown-eyed people learn fast, don't they? Boy, do brown-eyed people learn fast!"

And the brown-eyed people did learn fast that day. The day before, running through a pack of flash cards against a stop watch, a reading group of brown-eyed children had taken five and a half minutes to sound out the various phonic combinations on the cards. Now, the same children sped through the same card pack in less than half that time. A blue-eyed reading group had gone through the card pack in three minutes the day before. Today, wearing their blue collars, they took four minutes and eighteen seconds.

As in everything else during those two days, Jane had consciously aided the "superior" group, turning the cards faster, ignoring minor errors. With the "inferior" group, she had in-

sisted on absolute accuracy, giving them no help
at all. Still, even allowing for the difference her
own deliberate bias had made, she was convinced that there had been a real difference between the speed of each group on the two days.
"If nothing else," she says, "both groups went
through the pack much faster on the days they
were supposedly 'superior' than they ever had
before. And in everything else they did on those
two days, it was clear that the children that had
been labeled inferior were, in fact, behaving as
though they were inferior, while the 'superior'
children performed in a consistently superior
manner."

After the brown-eyed children had sped
through the phonic card pack that second day,
Jane congratulated them. "You went faster
than I ever had anyone go through the card
pack," she said, smiling at their excitement and
pleasure. "Why couldn't you get them yesterday?"

"We had those collars on," Donna Reddel
said. The others agreed.

"Oh," Jane said. "You think the collars kept
you—"

"We couldn't think with those collars on,"
Roy Wilson said excitedly. "My eyes just kept
going around and around."

"Oh," Jane said again, "and you couldn't think
as well with the collars on."

When the blue-eyed children, who had done
so well the day before, did poorly on the card

pack, Raymond spoke up. "I knew we weren't going to make it."

"What happened?" Jane asked.

"We went down," Rex Kozak said.

"Why? What were you thinking of?"

"This," said Rex, lifting his collar.

"Why?" Jane asked.

"It itches my neck."

"Oh," Jane said. "Do you think if we took it off, you'd do better?"

Rex looked at her and then shook his head. "No."

"Then it isn't the collar?"

"No."

"What is it?"

"Blue eyes," Raymond said.

"Well, we could take the collars off," Jane said, "but we can't change the color of our eyes, can we?"

"No," Raymond said glumly.

"I hate today," Jane said suddenly.

"You do? I hate it, too," Rex said with enthusiasm.

"Because I'm blue-eyed," Jane added.

"See, I am, too," Rex explained.

"It's not funny; it's not fun; it's not pleasant," Jane said emphatically. "This is a filthy, nasty word called 'discrimination.' We're treating people in a certain way because they are different from the rest of us. Is that fair?"

"No," they answered in unison.

"Nothing fair about it. We didn't say this was going to be a fair day, did we?"

"No."

"And it isn't. It's a horrid day."

Still, it was not as horrid as the day before. The brown-eyed children, perhaps because they remembered how it had felt, did not discriminate against their blue-eyed classmates with quite the same zeal as the latter had against them the previous day. There were no fights. Yet the blue-eyed children, having been treated as superior the previous day, reacted to their sudden fall from grace with the same depression, the same tension, the same anger as had their brown-eyed classmates. Raymond Hansen later put it succinctly. Of the first day, he said, "I felt like a king, like I ruled them brown-eyes. Like I was better than them. Happy." The second day, he said, "I felt down, unhappy, like I couldn't do anything, like I was tied up and couldn't get loose."

On both days of the exercise, Jane had the children draw pictures of her. Without exception, the "superior" group saw her as happy and smiling, while the "inferior" group portrayed her as a frowning scold. In pictures the children drew of themselves each day, the differences in the way they felt were dramatized even more strongly. Roy Wilson's drawing of himself on his "inferior" day was half the size

88

of his drawing on his "superior" day. Hairless, mouth turned down, his clothes lacking completely in detail, his first day's image of himself was eloquent testimony to his confused sense of depression. In contrast, on the second day, the large, well-drawn figure sported a happy smile, a checked shirt, a turned-up nose, and short, blond hair.

Eyelashes and eyebrows appeared along with a happy smile in Donna's picture of herself on the day she was treated as superior. They had been missing from the previous day's drawing. Laurie Mayer saw herself with tears streaming from her brown eyes, her hands in tight fists on her "inferior" day.

Milton Wolthoff, a quiet, blue-eyed boy who had done little to call attention to himself on either day, drew the most spectacularly different pictures of himself. On his "superior" day, his image all but filled the bright yellow page, and above his happy, smiling face, an angelic figure, also smiling, danced on his head waving a sign reading, "Happy Days." Colored balloons and streamers surrounded the angel. On his "inferior" day, Milton appeared at the very bottom of a solid black page, a tiny miserable figure with a devil, complete with horns and pitchfork, atop his head.

John Benttine, the boy who had hit Russell Ring on his day on the bottom, drew himself tied by his blue collar to a post, holding in his hand a sign obviously addressed to Jane. "You

crab," it read. The sign in his hand the next day
read simply, "Happy." Raymond Hansen drew
himself as pink and smiling the day he had felt
like a king. On the other day, he drew himself
as a Negro.

Toward the end of that second day, Jane was
called to the office. When she returned to the
classroom, she told the children that Russell
was in the hospital, that they had located the
pin, that he was all right, but that he would
stay in the hospital for a day or so. Then she
asked them to come down to the front of the
room. They gathered around the low stool on
which she sat, seating themselves on the floor
or on the front desks.

"What did you people who are wearing blue
collars find out today?" she asked when all was
quiet.

"I know what they felt like yesterday," Raymond said.

"I do, too," Greg said emphatically.

"How did they feel yesterday?" Jane asked.

"Like a dog on a leash," Greg said.

"Like you're chained up in a prison and they
threw the key away," Raymond said.

"Should the color of some other person's eyes
have anything to do with how you treat them?"
Jane asked.

There was a unanimous "No."

"All right, then should the color of their
skin?"

This time the "No" was louder.

"Should you judge people by the color of their skin?"

"No."

"You're going to say that today," Jane said, "and this week, and probably all the time you're in this room. You'll say, 'No-o-o, Missus Elliott,'" she chanted in a mocking, singsong way. "Every time I ask that question. Then, when you see a black man or an Indian or someone different from you walking down the street, are you going to say, 'Ha, ha, look at that silly-looking thing?'"

Their answer was almost indignant. "No!" they shouted, and then Raymond and Donna together picked up Jane's previous intonation and, the others joining in, they all said, "No-o-o, Missus Elliott," with sarcastic sweetness.

Jane laughed and then turned serious again. "Does it make any difference whether their skin is black or white?"

"No."

"Or yellow? Or red?"

"No."

"Is that how you decide whether people are good or bad?"

"No."

"Is that what *makes* people good or bad?"

"No."

"Let's take these collars off."

Greg, fumbling for the pin, said, "I'd like to just jerk it off if I could."

In a minute, the collars were off—all except Brian Saltou's. Brian sat on a desk ignoring the others as they began handing their collars to Jane.

"What would you like to do with them?" Jane asked.

"Burn them!" Raymond said.

"Throw them away!" Greg shouted.

"Go ahead!" Jane shouted back at him.

There was a rush for the wastebasket and through the noise of excited chatter a boy's voice could be heard advising, "Don't eat the pin like Russell did!" Jane winced.

When all the other blue-eyed children had thrown away their collars, Brian still sat on the desk top wearing his. "Aren't you going to take your collar off, Brian?" Jane asked.

He shook his head.

"Why not?"

"I like it," he said, smiling slightly.

"You like it," Jane repeated. Brian nodded. "Everyone else has taken his collar off, but you're going to keep yours on." He nodded again. "Why?"

"I just like it, that's all," he said.

"All right," Jane said. "Keep it on."

Instantly, his hands went to the collar. He took it off, folding it neatly.

"Don't you want to throw it away?" Jane asked him.

"No."

"Why not?"

"I'm going to keep it. I'm going to take it home."

"And what do you plan to do with it at home?"

"I'm going to put it on my dog."

"You're going to put it on your dog?"

"Yeah," Brian said. "I'll put it on him for a tail. He just has a little-bitty screw tail."

Jane paused for a moment. "I think you'd better throw the collar away, Brian," she said firmly. "All the others have, and I think you'd better, too."

Brian looked at her as though to decide if he could defy her any longer. Then he slid off the desk and went to the wastebasket, and while the other children, rejoicing in their reunion, struggled to get nearer to each other, the boys with their arms around each other, the girls hugging each other in relief, Brian fiercely tore, bit, and ripped the collar until it was in shreds. Finally, he returned to the group, but ignoring the fact that all were now on the floor, he perched himself again on the desk, with them but not a part of them.

"Now you know a little bit more than you knew at the beginning of the week," Jane was saying.

"Yes," they answered.

"A lot more," Raymond added.

"Do you know a little bit more than you wanted to?"

Their exuberance ran over, and in a single,

jeering voice, they chanted, "Ye-e-es, Missus Elliott!"

"This isn't an easy way to learn it, is it?"

Once again, they chanted, "No-o-o, Missus Elliott!"

Jane, pretending anger, shouted at them, "Oh, will you stop that!"

They broke up with laughter, the boys rolling backwards away from her, the girls clutching each other, tears in their eyes. It took a few minutes before they had begun to settle down again.

"Okay," Jane said, "now let's all sit down here together, blue eyes and brown eyes. Does it make any difference what color your eyes are?"

"No!" they shouted, beginning to laugh again.

"Okay," she said, smiling at them, "now are you back together again?"

"Yes!" they shouted, and the boys, arms around each other, began swaying back and forth like a row of students in the cheering section of a football stadium.

"Does that feel better?"

"Yes!"

Sheila, Susan, and Julie, the three inseparables, sat close to each other, Sheila in the middle, with tears of relief and joy streaming down her face; the others comforting her. "What's the matter, Sheila?" Jane asked, and Sheila laughed and cried and wiped at her eyes.

"She's crying," Julie said, on the verge of tears herself.

"Feel better now?" Jane asked, and Sheila managed to nod. "Miserable situation, isn't it?" Jane asked. Sheila sniffed and nodded again, and the other girls hugged her.

"Does that feel like being home again, girls?" Jane asked, smiling at them.

This time they all three nodded, sniffing.

"Okay," Jane said, "who knows a song?"

"'Paw-Paw Patch'!" someone shouted.

"All right," Jane said, and then singing, "'Where, O where is sweet little Sheila?'" started them all laughing again.

"'Where, O where is sweet little Sheila? Where, O where is sweet little Sheila?'" they sang, laughing and pointing at Sheila, who laughed and cried and wiped at her eyes.

"'Way down yonder in the paw-paw patch!'" they shouted.

"Let's do it!" Jane cried, standing up. "Everybody get a partner!"

They scrambled to their feet, milling around, choosing partners.

"Do we have to have girls for partners, Mrs. Elliott?" Roy asked pleadingly.

Jane laughed out loud. "No, Roy, you don't have to have girls."

The boys cheered lustily and paired off. The girls hugged each other, jumping up and down. Quickly a double row was formed, but with Russell Ring gone, they were one boy short. The extra boy, of course, was Brian.

"Come on, Brian," Jane said, still laughing.

"I'm sorry, but it looks like you're stuck with me." Brian grimaced, grinned, and took her hand. They were still singing and dancing when the bell rang.

IX

In the weeks immediately following those two days in February, 1970, Jane Elliott was struck by the undeniable improvement in the work of her students. "Four of them in particular," she says, "Rex Kozak, Sheila Schaefer, Julie Smith, and Greg Johanns, simply flew. It was like nothing I've ever seen. They just caught fire. When the class took Stanford Achievement Tests in April, I simply couldn't wait for the machine-scored results; I corrected the tests myself to see if what I had observed was true. It was. Rex Kozak, for example, had gained two years in reading ability and four and five years in everything else. In just a single year."

Sheila Schaefer had also gained two full years in reading ability. Walking to recess with her one day, Jane told her how well she was doing. "Your grades have done nothing but go

up, up, up, ever since Discrimination Day," she
said. "What happened to you?"

Sheila smiled happily. "I found out I was just
as good as you said I was. You told me I could
do anything, and I can. *I'm smart!*"

Jane is somewhat at a loss to explain the
relevance of Discrimination Day to learning,
because, as she puts it, "I had been telling Sheila
and all the other children how capable they
were since the beginning of the school year. Yet
it wasn't until after the exercise that they really
began to soar. I suppose the sharp contrast between the kind of work they did on one day and
the next might have something to do with it,
but I really don't know. I wish someone could
tell me how to get these results without putting children through such torture."

As in previous years, Jane's students continued to bring up the lessons they had learned
through the exercise, to apply them to other situations, and to exhibit a sharp interest in anything that smacked even remotely of discrimination. "I think," Jane says, "if it has done
nothing else for the children who have been
through it, the exercise has widened their
worlds. It has made them look beyond themselves. It has helped them relate to other people. I think, too, it has helped teach them
not to take at face value everything everybody
says. It's made them think about things in a way
they haven't before, with a kind of healthy skep-
ticism. And I think it makes children feel dif-

ferently about themselves. It must, because their performance changes, academically and socially."

Once the exercise had begun, the children, caught up in the intense, conflicting emotions of the new and absorbing experience, had all but ignored the presence of the television film crews. Once it was over, they awaited the broadcast of the documentary with unconcealed impatience. It came, finally, on May 11, broadcast over the ABC Television Network under the title "The Eye of the Storm." Most of Riceville watched it.

Some Riceville adults were put off by a bit of narration in the first few minutes of the program, a line that described the community as "relatively poor." But the children in Jane's class were all but mesmerized at seeing themselves on television. Writing about it the next day in class, most told how moved their parents and relatives had been. "My mother almost cried" was a much-repeated line. Some of the children were surprised at how they had looked. "I didn't know how unhappy I was the second day," Raymond Hansen wrote. For all, living through the experience a second time had called up many of the emotions they had experienced on those two days three months earlier.

Brian Saltou, who had held out against Jane's discriminatory statements and actions, was, of course, a sort of star of the program. For weeks

99

afterwards, he walked tall and proud. Rex Kozak told the class of being called a "movie star" by children on the school bus. Jane asked him if he minded. "It was fun," he said, grinning broadly.

A deluge of letters descended on the school after the broadcast, and the class put up a map of the United States and stuck pins in it to indicate the source of each of them. By the end of the school year, forty-four states were represented. "I read most of the letters to the class," Jane says, "all but the worst of the racist ones. More than ninety-five percent of the mail was favorable, but I felt the children should know that not everyone agreed with what we had done or even what they had learned.

"The morning after the broadcast, in fact, a man had called the school from somewhere in the South and left a message for me: 'I saw your phony sideshow on TV last night. Garbage, garbage, garbage. Fake, fake, fake.'

"I told the children, and we discussed what he might have meant. In the end, we concluded that he must have thought the exercise had been made up, that the children were simply acting out roles that had been assigned to them, knowing all the time it was a sort of game; that the whole thing had been, in effect, a play presented as reality. It was obvious, of course, that he didn't approve of the lesson. But this idea that the children were pretending to feel what they expressed, that they were acting, either for me or for the television cameras; that they could not actually have believed themselves to be inferior or superior so quickly after having been told it was a classroom exercise—this sense of disbelief was present in many of the letters we received. Reading them, I remembered how difficult it had been for me to accept it when I myself had seen it happen the first time.

"I have no final explanation for it—this absolutely real acceptance of the roles assigned them. And I don't blame other people for finding it hard to believe. But it has happened just that way each time I have done it. If it proves anything, I suppose it proves how susceptible human beings—and particularly children—are to a voice of authority.

"But even more pernicious, it also illustrates how the results of discrimination tend to create and confirm prejudice. It's a simple enough equation: choose a group, discriminate against it, force it by your discrimination to look and act inferior, and then point to the way it looks and acts as proof of its inferiority. A man who has been forced to bow and scrape will look to the outsider like a man who wants to bow and scrape. Eventually, he may even look that way to himself. A child who has been denied a decent education will become an uneducated adult. To those who didn't see—or refuse to recognize—the denial, he will seem simply stupid.

"I have asked each class that has gone through this exercise why they believed me when I said that one group or the other was inferior. The answer has always been the same. They believed me at first, tentatively, because I said it was so, because I was the teacher. Later, they believed me because they *saw* it was so. And, of course, they *had* seen it. Didn't the 'inferior' group do inferior work? Weren't they constantly having to be corrected? Didn't they become sulky, inattentive, and unhappy? And isn't that precisely what we all do when we discriminate against Negroes in employment and then castigate them as unable to do anything but sweep floors?"

To the racist letters that Jane received and read to her class, the children's reaction was healthy and intelligent. "They decided, reluctantly, I think, that there were adults who simply didn't know what they now knew," Jane says. "It gave them an even greater sense of the importance of the lesson, I suspect. And I hope it reinforced their determination to think for themselves."

As for Jane Elliott, her life, too, has been changed somewhat by the broadcasting of her lesson in discrimination. In succeeding months, she appeared on a number of television programs, explaining again what she had done and why. She addressed several professional and educational groups at their request. In the fall of 1970, she was chosen to be a member of a panel of the White House Conference on

Children and Youth. Word of her classroom exercise has spread far from the classroom.

In Riceville itself, the reaction both to the television program and to Jane's exercise has been overwhelmingly favorable. There have been some critics. Some, motivated by a frank antagonism to Negroes, have complained privately that she should not be teaching school children that Negroes are the equal of whites. Others, annoyed perhaps by the sudden notoriety of someone who grew up in their own small town, have grumbled that she is getting too big for her boots. Such responses could have been anticipated.

But there has been little but praise of the exercise from educators and psychologists. In this category, Jane is surely her own severest critic. "I've wondered, each time I've done it, if what I'm doing is right," she says. "I've worried, each time, about the possibility of hurting a child. And I've wished, each time, that someone would show me another way, a better way, a less painful way to teach children that discrimination is wrong. What I hope, of course, is that these children will retain at least something of what they've learned in these lessons, that when they become involved, later on, in situations that feel similar to the one they experienced here, they will recognize, consciously or unconsciously, what the other person must be feeling, and pull back.

"But more than that, I hope they will retain

the knowledge gained in this painful way that
discrimination based on race or color or religion
or any other arbitrary difference between people is illogical and irrational, that it makes no
sense, and even worse, that unless they think
hard about it, it can be imposed on them from
the outside. I hope they know now and for all
time that just because someone says something
is true, just because society acts as though a
fact were established, doesn't make it so. I want
them to think, to reason, to question. I hope I've
given them at least a starting tool to work in
that direction.

"I'm not so naïve that I think this single exercise is going to change the world—or even
Riceville," Jane says. "But we have to start
somewhere if we hope to live in a society free
of the irrationality of racism. I'm a teacher. I
work with children. This is simply where I
started."

ABOUT THE AUTHOR

As a writer, television producer, and film director, William Peters has focused much of his work on the crucial issues of our times. Among them, the broad subject of race relations has assumed a central position. During more than twenty years of interest and involvement in what is surely America's most explosive domestic problem, he has written scores of magazine articles and two previous books, as well as producing a number of television documentaries, on various aspects of the race question.

The Southern Temper, published in 1959, was a critically acclaimed study of the then-current racial crisis in the South. *For Us, The Living,* written with Mrs. Medgar Evers, widow of the murdered Mississippi civil rights leader, appeared in 1967 to be hailed as "one of the most significant stories to emerge from the Negro revolution in America."

As a producer for the distinguished television series, "CBS Reports," Mr. Peters wrote, produced, and directed a number of outstanding documentaries, including *Mississippi and the Fifteenth Amendment, The Priest and the Politician, Segregation: Northern-Style,* and two of the three parts of the prize-winning *Storm Over the Supreme Court.*

In 1966, he spent three months with a film crew in East Africa as a producer-director of the four-hour ABC Television presentation, *Africa,* broadcast in the fall of 1967. His most recent television documentary for ABC was *The Eye of the Storm,* a brilliant and highly-praised half-hour program whose filming covered a part of the subject matter of this book.

Born in San Francisco in 1921, Mr. Peters has lived and worked in many parts of the United States. He is as much at home in the Negro section of Ruleville, Mississippi as in the classrooms of Riceville, Iowa. From hundreds of places as dissimilar as these have come his revealing reports on a nation at war with itself over the specious issue of color.

M